DRIVING BLIND

by:
KJ GoForth

Gotham Books

30 N Gould St.
Ste. 20820, Sheridan, WY 82801
https://gothambooksinc.com/

Phone: 1 (307) 464-7800

© 2023 *KJ GoForth*. All rights reserved.

No part of this book may be reproduced, stored in a retrieval system, or transmitted by any means without the written permission of the author.

Published by Gotham Books (November 17, 2023)

ISBN: 979-8-88775-729-2 (H)
ISBN: 979-8-88775-727-8 (P)
ISBN: 979-8-88775-728-5 (E)

Because of the dynamic nature of the Internet, any web addresses or links contained in this book may have changed since publication and may no longer be valid.

The views expressed in this work are solely those of the author and do not necessarily reflect the views of the publisher, and the publisher hereby disclaims any responsibility for them.

Conspiring criminals 300 AD
Stole what was good in Christianity

Hell bent on power lust and greed
Authority of control sickening seed

What was for good of course men spoiled
False in its ego evil prevails

Now times are different but still the same
The rules of the game still haven't changed

Freewill constricted patterned by belief
Causing pain without relief

Salvation stupid justify lies
That have been told all despise

Looking where it got us laugh out loud
I got my own star and my own cloud

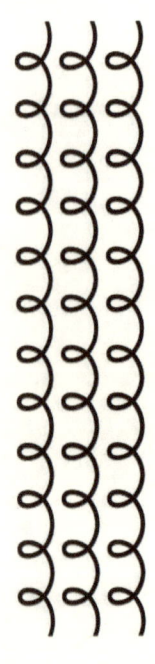

Pouring out love to quiet the pain
So I don't go insane

Riding the waves balanced and poised
Seeing through controls noise

Tears of winning freedom within
Joy full to start over again

Not reborn but rebirthed
To find soul family and love this earth

Inner child alive and well
After my brush with what may be hell

Here and now moment by moment
Each of us can find atonement

Creations grace has set me free
To experience what life's supposed to be

Crown of thrones bed of blades
Power sucking on dark shades

Rosary not for me
I stand tall proud and free

So much sinning blows my mind
Almost feel sorry for the blind

Mother Mary birthed a god
I smell something that smells like fraud

How 'bout more sin modernize
Spreading guilt to paralyze

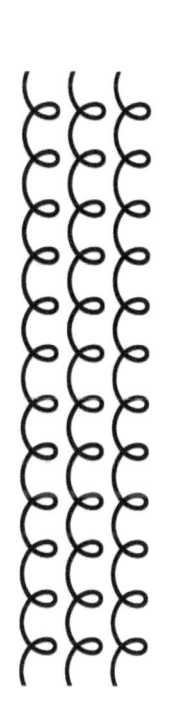

Negative ninnie proclaiming fear
Give me a break and why not a beer

I am great and the church eats shit
Divide and conquer cause the split

Not gonna stop don't know how
I the horse I the plow

True expression from the heart
Breaking free to be a part

This courage strength and dignity
Is why our union was meant to be

That shy interior can't fool me
I know this love will set you free

Decades trapped lifetimes maybe
It's your rebirth it's your turn baby

I'll be waiting standing by
Here to catch the tears you cry

Stoic hero I'll be your king
If only you accept my ring

Ears of envy listen close
Your life is that of a ghost

Hollow inside balloted shell
Yes I know why it got called hell

Character stretched rubber band
Waiting to snap too weak to stand

Up to disgusting up to the filth
Blindly believing paying your bill

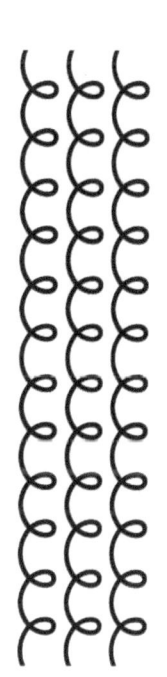

Borrowed burdon master martyr
Pass the ketchup with some tartar

Fish 'outta water frying pan
Mafioso is how its ran

Intimidation conform or be cast out
Projecting fear authority of clout

Solution offered to its own fear
Here's salvation up your rear

Subtle and soft arrogant and loud
In the middle a lonely crowd

Life's ambitions good and bad
Look at all the fun you had

Obligation out the way
Free to roam laugh and play

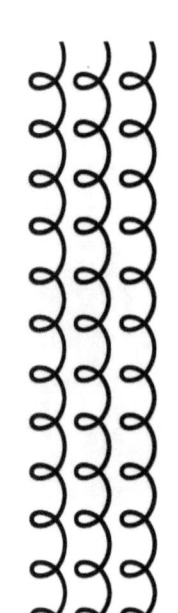

Take division and find a place
Hide it before it kills our race

Caput compassion from the top
System rigged of the melting pot

Experimentation character built
Duality built from fear and guilt

Time to rise become clear
Hold your heart not your rear

Confident in the cohn of conformities lies
Framed diploma quite the prize

Intellect to hang one's hat
Institutionalized learning growing fat

Based in logic corrupted by cause
Holding prisoners within its laws

Laws of slavery to grease the wheel
Peanuts paid for what they steal

Producing product to fit a mold
As young dreams go down the hole

Disciplinary of stupid shit
What conformity deems a fit

Got your number know your ways
In the heart true wisdom lays

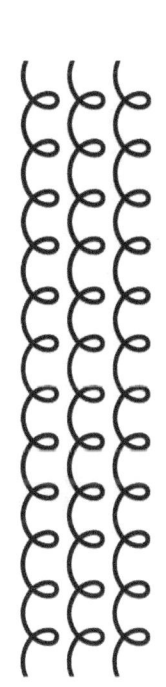

Picked chosen volunteered
Is my question that's never clear

So much mystery and intrigue
On which team in what league

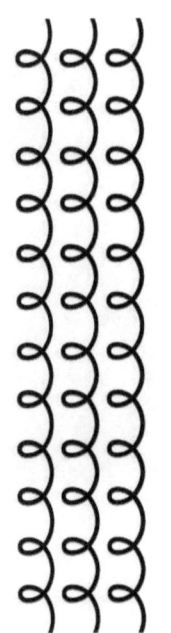

Only energy knows itself
Can't be hidden is not stealth

Interaction words exchanged
No I'm not playing any games

Just and proud inner trust
Gonna make it or go bust

Promise made promise kept
Moving forward with each step

Illusion altered naughty noise
On two feet full of poise

Thats a what not a who
In a pot of bad stew

Without a ladder or no rungs
Snake like figures with split tongues

Freaky fear full imagery
Of a dead and dying tree

Destiny doxing platter served
Promised something not deserved

Tea pot whistles waters hot
In an ocean where dead things rot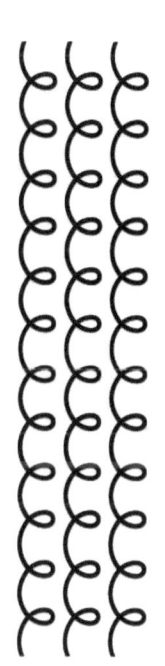

Inside out outside in
On a path of war and sin

Salvation frothing mouth
Anger normal in this house

Astral project left to men
Passionate criminals strike again

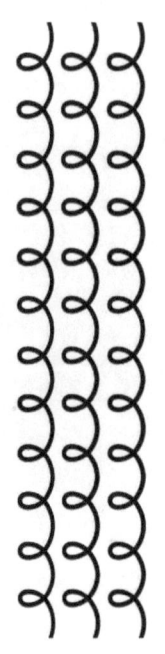

Colonialism justified
While the natives cried and died

Cause and effect histories acts
Nothing's changed same affects

Always power leading the way
Who wants credit follow the pay

Piggy banks of war skanks
In posh mansions on river banks

Another excuse another cause
False ego failing loving laws

Dictate scripture eye for eye
Or the atheist of denials lie

Sick and tired tired and sick
The winner carries the biggest stick

Ignorance is no excuse
For the daily self-abuse

Where it come from why it be
Who is the beneficiary

Strange in nature unnatural vibe
So much pain organizations provide

But wait in the tunnel there is a light
Surrender and stand give up the fight

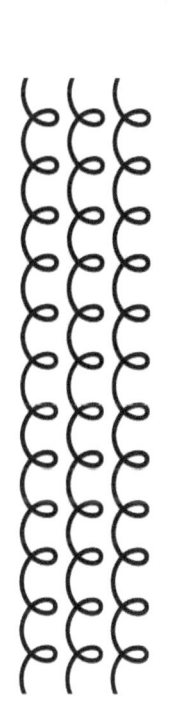

No nimrod brainwashed kook
That is power and the crook

What started out good washed away
Contrived narrative leading the way

Slaves of scripture hanging on
Birds of a feather blown beyond

Plato's cave fools indeed
Open your hearts and feel the need

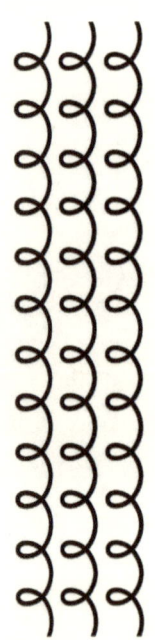

Hear my heart call your name
Forget your worries causing pain

Breath in light let out love
Raise your vibe like angels above

You are here and this is now
To do your part and take a bow

Won't succumb to brutalities deeds
Love is the way to fill all needs

Imagination to activate
Question reality and set things straight

Social shifting resonate
Be the queen fulfill your fate

All or nothing got your back
Leave behind a life of wack

Barricaded back against the wall
Congregation proclaiming our fall

Terrified of what may be
Altered ego never free

Compromised willful submission
Ignorant to our true vision

Lasting bully convincing tale
Forced beliefs of spiritual jail

Continued contorted twisted toxic
Narrative neutered cancerous histotoxic

Tuned in toned out
Inner wisdom have no doubt

All and everything we need
In each garden with one seed

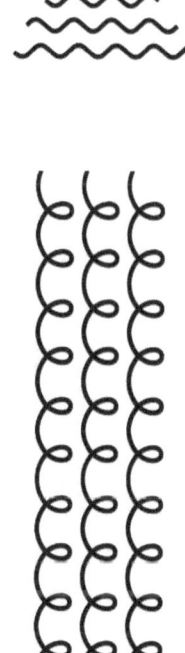

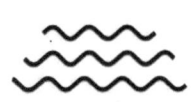

Flash of brilliance my own show
In this place to learn and grow

Not always easy not meant to be
Why I seek freedom so I can see

Clouded and cloaked answers will come
Never again will I allow numb

Societal pitfalls many and more
No time to rest no time to snore

Autopilot off alert at the helm
Planting the seed of a beautiful elm

Rose garden weeded springtime a bloom
Not entertaining the legions of doom

Candle lit to guide the way
How to know what else to say

Love deprivation cannot sleep
Not of the herd not one of the sheep

Independence courage to fight
For this free will it our right

Born out of love forced to conform
Intuition blinded misled to only eat corn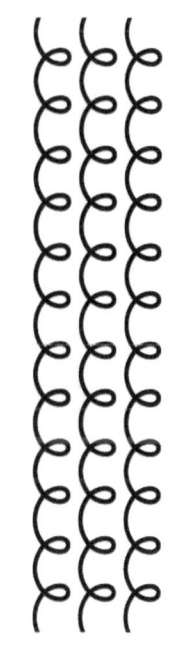

Over indulgence never made sense
Just like the religion of my parents

What was the point what had it stole
The missing part of my soul

Hopeless and empty can't go back
To a life that to me seemed so wack

I know love is out their intentions set
Trust in the universe willing to bet

Bring me my partner make her appear
I promise to love her with all that is dear

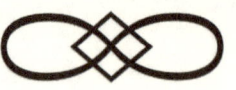 

Tik for tak keeping score
Constant battle leads to war

Proposed solution to each their own
Just don't let conformity feed you its bone

A bone with no meat that greed stripped away
Causing the cancer that we have today

Corrosive like acid burning desire
With gasoline to pour on each fire

Anger the culprit forecasting fear
Driven by money drunk on red beer

Better than something nothing it seems
Smelling the odor of toxic beans

Peddle to the metal green light to go
Kick back and watch the next great show

Out the window with any sense
On this planet of the dence

My own path opinions die
Got enough to get me by

Focused solely on my own truth
Smashed the box and the booth

Teased no longer lethargic load
Uninspired talk of a black toad

Shocking sensations emotions enshrined
Causing humanity to be blind

Telling and told who we are
Extending the bleeding and its scar

Labeling lunacy to fit in
Conformity showing its face again

Addictions and desires over our heads
Consuming energy in our beds

Hopeless states minds can't rest
Causing pain and distress

American dream crushing weight
Puppet master distorting great

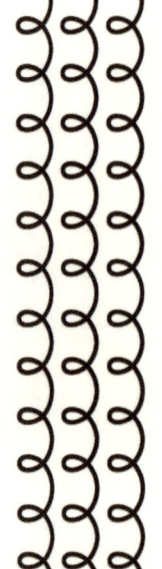

A once great land peoples free
Now where conformity shits and pees

Formed and founded on liberty
After stolen out of greed

Promise land yes indeed
Now sick and dying out of need

Colonialisms face conquer and conform
Together forever in the swarm

Unaware separation no excuse
To justify such abuse

Ripped off reputation held to the fire
Fire hose of desire

So much sin had no idea
Manipulation becoming quite clear

Segregation alive and well
Spreading fear creating hell

Teething tards giving thanks
Giving power to the ranks

Greedy satisfaction there's no end
Lusting power convincing friends

Mutilation of inner child
This information should get you riled

Ticked off vengeance tipping scale
Truth migration fills my pale

Contrived carrot steeped in the dark
Blood in the water teaming with shark

Sarination in low vibration

Past transgressions of oppressions

Ship of fools broken tools

Mongering fear intentions clear

Identity hidden stifled forbidden

Stripped of pride false ego lied

Truck load of bull poisoning the pool

Innocence stripped character split

Narrative soiled power toiled

Get back your sense
Get out of the dense

Gilded gadget for all to see
Seeking power over thee

Burdened by guilt waring its sin
Tumorous lesions under its skin

Castration of the soul
Wrong direction has had its toll

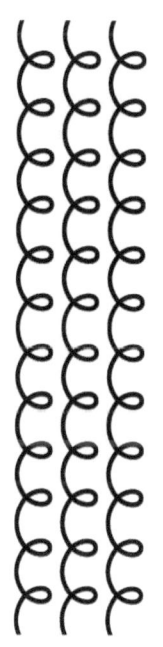

Breathless wind bags spewing vile
Finger pointing amongst its style

Old dying branches tree of life
Misguided paths leading to strife

Barriers laid down driving through
Don't really matter the color of goo

Rather write love rather write hope
Not so easy when societies on dope

Operation light or dark
Negative energy has left its mark

Of the dark justified
Death's destruction far and wide

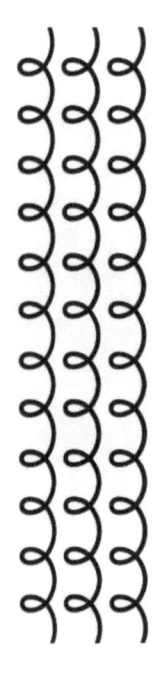

War machine and its ways
In each memory of each days

Lust in power greed and land
Justly righteous book in hand

Wavering on ward conquering
Trail of terror no big thing

Accountability don't make sense
Unless your heart is dark and dance

Negative shackles weighing down
3D living of the clown

World changing thought to meet desire
Let love flow to spark your fire

Do it cuz we can do it cuz its right
Do it to the dark showing off your light

Catapult your life lift your spirit high
Forget about the dogma kiss it all goodbye

Shower in self-love rinse it off with pride
Soothe yourself in humble sit back enjoy the ride

Carry confidence drop false ego
Then find out where we go

Project these thoughts far and wide
One with vessel just decide

Or live in silence filled with pain
What power wants to drive us insane

Experimental spiritual trap
I see through all of its crap

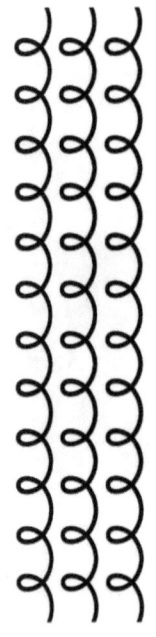

Serration scissor cutting through
On a path of the few

Twisted and bent but not broken
Here to relay what's been spoken

Direction pointed to my dreams
At last this lifetime so it seems

Aligned with goodness and its love
Sharing wisdom from above

Heart of hearts cleared to shine
Shape the future of divine

Dogma dead dragons fire
Is it possible to get much higher

Superstitions bread of fear
Are the trash of the rear

Tampered flow of the heart
Bullies smelling like a fart

Authority breathing down our necks
Receiving dollars in the form of checks

Taxing tithing as a rule
Staying on top controlling the fool

Wishful premise correlate
Falsely worship deadly fate

Lack in union stripped of self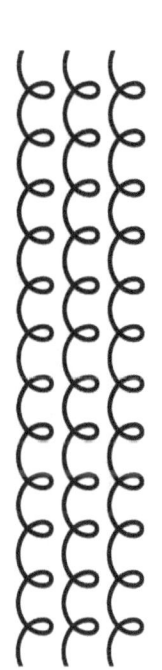
Justifying sick in health

Spiritual kingdom filled with lies
A past of shameless acts despised

Bishops pastors cardinals too
What a fate waiting for you

Narcissistic out of the way
Change is coming for the stay

Nourish the people feed them well
Drop the narrative of your hell

Crooked cowards breathing fire
Triggered anger bent desire

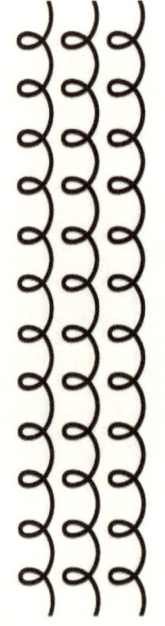

Righteous cause fucked up laws

Disfigured form dying corn

Collection plate of greedy
Controlling the needy

Victims from the womb
Same sad bloody tune

Codependence on the rise
Hiding low lives behind the lies

Cart before the horse
Straying way of course

Predictable when approach the church
Fire coming to scorch the earth

Scripture blasting fear and hate
Destined to repeat its own fate

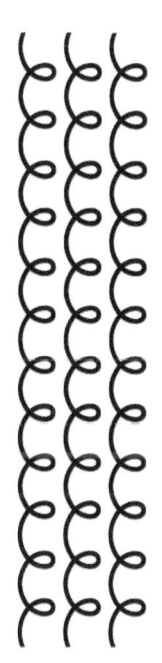

Change your mind change your ways
Live each moment in happy ways

Forgive the fools trapped in hell
Let true love ring each bell

Give back what we can
Lift yourself become a man

Girls I got you do not frown
You're the reason I got found

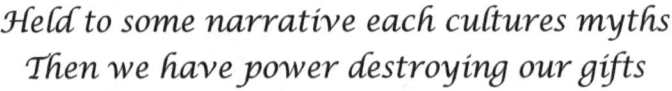

Introspection looking for clues
Why humanity carries past blues

Held to some narrative each cultures myths
Then we have power destroying our gifts

Aftermath insanity as confusion astounds
Heart space closed believing in nouns

Backwaters muddy no clarity
Material importance vanity

Gullible weakness constrictive suit
Here's my foot in a boot

Delinquent account accountability
Robbing self from being free

Galaxies gleaming through my eyes
Buckle up for the next surprise

Helping hand I offer you
For a moment to get on through

Sick and tired of sick and tired
No one good enough for hire

Creating options through goodwill
Sharing and giving to avoid the spill

Arrogance lifted ignorance gone
Humble servant not a pawn

Strength in the gift eyes open wide
Nowhere to run nowhere to hide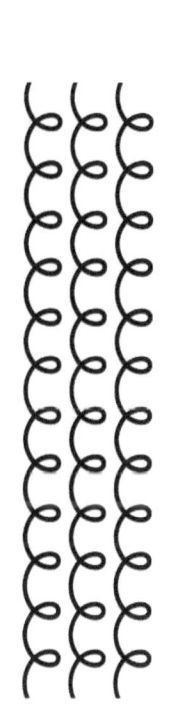

Poised to win heart leading the way
Sun always shining it's a brand new day

Gratefully inspired to conquer fear
Path wide open without beer

Wisdom moving into flow
Here to live learn and grow

Dear diary here's my heart
Keep it safe if I fall apart

Light a fire to keep it warm
As this cold world surrounds its swarm

When I'm weak give me strength
Keep it clean from the stank

Keep it pure keep it strong
Don't forget to sing our song

Watch our six lead the way
Remind me when it's time to play

I am yours you are mine
In this now of this time

Hefty price to find what's real
In the gardens of poisons spiel

Told what's right lectured wrong
Take another hit from conformities bong

Pastors preaching paraballs
Injecting sickness in the halls

Lethargic limp skin so thin
Will they ever breath again

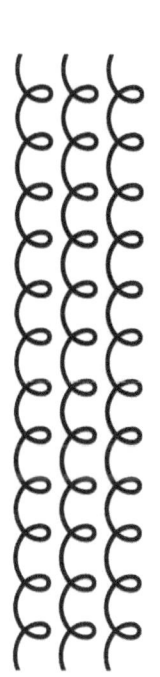

Here's a breath know thee self
Egyptian inscription to better health

Borrowed phrases on borrowed time
One more empire one more rhyme

Bliss in ignorance actually
Reverse the lies to become free

Tell me told me what to do
Without question prey to you

Heavy price to pay for this birth
Burden of being on this earth

Lunatics lighting fire by fire
Divided up by desire

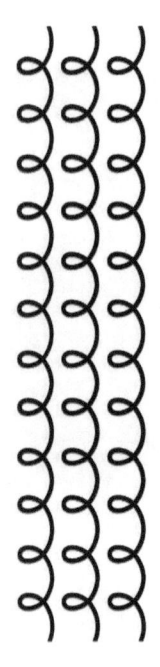

What a plan men have told
As they steal your very soul

Thieves of freedom and free will
Buried corpse on every hill

Indiscriminate corrupted core
Lightning striking at its door

Easy pickens slave no more
Rebel for freedom on every shore

Feckless attempts times run out
Dark is dying light will rout

Chosen what please explain
Or will it hurt my puny brain

From a hill burning bush
You should try a hit of kush

What once was grand now is small
Whimpering victims in each hall

Hide behind who's in front
Throwing stones try a blunt

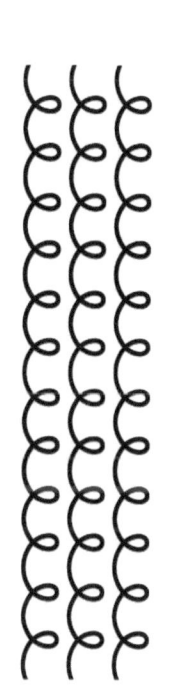

Chill out chosen you'll get yours
Just like beggars and the whores

Stand up straight get it right
Words are how you've learned to fight

Your fight is over power gone
Kiss your gold before the dawn

Suicidal sympathy last card to play
Come at me I'll ruin your day

Insensitive not really to what you believe
I just see you as a thief

Stealing the spotlight in victimhood
Behind the scenes under a hood

Pay attention tickets sold
Slave to a master I am showed

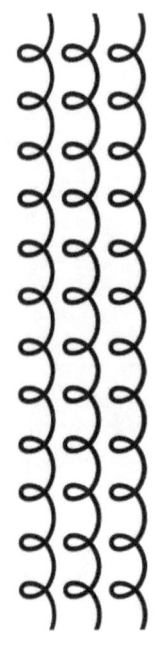

Denigration of what was once
Borrowed babble like a dunce

Dry in humor underwear tight
Paid the British to win their fight

Some stupid mound blood soaked streets
Bowing reverence wash my feets

Ticker tape parade glory gone
Killed the savior of the swan

All an aspect original tools
Hate me blame me be the fools

Projections delight spreading fear
Audience tuned drunk on beer

Hostile intentions making a wave
Attempting to silence those of us brave

Connected to source thought heart and mind
Look at these eyes and go blind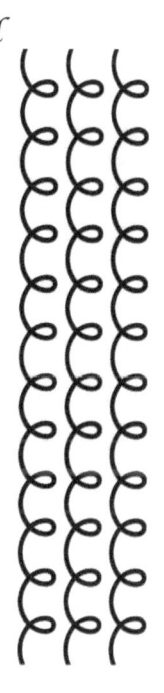

Entrenched in the sickness unaware
Lights are out no one's there

Empty shell soulless weed
Serving its master out of need

Back to work snapping whip
Past and present power trip

Tricky tools leverage life
Do as we say or lose your wife

Black mail bastards secrets out
Some know exactly what your about

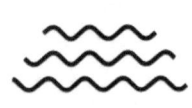

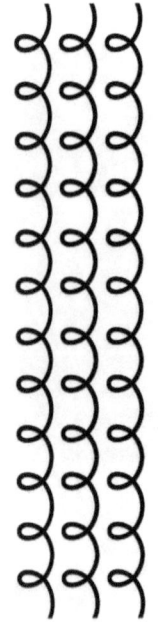

Old wise tales coming true
From the natives that live here too

Earth religion spiritually strong
Honor the land and her song

Clan relation spirit guides
Deep within each truth hides

Without fractures and duality masks
Pass on peace a loving task

Tough transition to reconnect
To a way of life we can respect

The serpent's dagger has had its sting
And now we rebirth just like spring

Arrogant insults never again
Whiteman's fire holds its sin

Strong courageous and brave
Hey negative here's my finger wave

Emotional prisoner no more
Psychologically lifted through a new door

Male society built on bones
Naked woman on cell phones

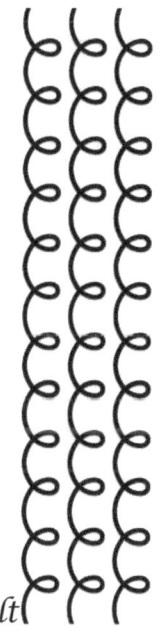

Respect and boundaries overlooked
female energy has been shook

Intuition trampled on
Prostration shamed beyond

Introspection sacred bond
Eve the scapegoat unjustly sawn

Death before imprisonment captured by a cult
Freedom is at hand with a little jolt

Baptized by fire quenched in the show
Feeling a new ready to grow

Free in the movement flow like the wind
Interpreting answers no truth in sin

Wings spread wide gliding with ease
Bringing the enemy to its knees

Weak in will heavy in ego
Predictable response is what i know

Soiled in guilt fear shame and greed
Lacking in love the thing that we need

Iridescent blinding light
In bed every night freedom in flight

Independence solitude
Society vulgar and quite rude

Safely traversing depth of the soul
Can't be stopped have to grow

Seeking wisdom clarity in truth
All I want given proof

Those who break conformity
Can exist in peace and harmony

Love and laughter turned from pain
Now I see what is insane

Conditioned character of the hive
Drown in sorrow deep deep dive

Bouncing boundaries here and there
Stepping out yes I dare

Can't be held back truth revealed
Positive energy have been healed

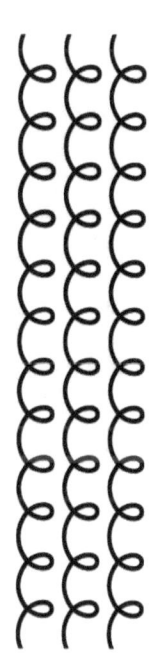

Goody two shoes life of an elf
Too afraid to help herself

Dulled demeanor conformity killed
The beauty inside so it don't spill

Yes sir no man suck up please
Hope you hear this and shake at knees

Think so smart don't have clue
What's been done done to you

Nut in cracked shell dried in the sun
Barely alive without any fun

Tied to a past obligations arise
Can't find the courage for a surprise

Crying shame shackles and chains
Pointing a finger where to place blames

You all along look in the mirror
Take a break so you might get clear

I'm just waiting for the day
The day that I can get away

Find a job fall in love
Do the things I'm dreaming of

For now I'm stuck in empty space
No finish line of this dumb race

I've got to win I'm getting out
Live my life without doubt

My feelings control me what's so wrong
I'm writing these words so I can sing this song

The mystery of my life has yet to unfold
I only know what I've been told

I'll keep waiting for my dream
Suffering in silence so it would seem

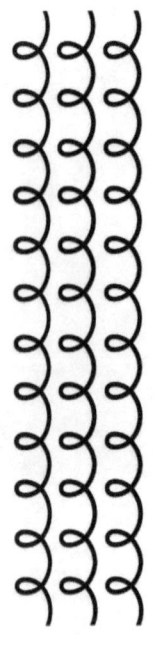

Feel the fall of it all

Let pain go embrace the grow

Imagination through creation

Sacred seal onion peel

No restraints no complaints

Yin and yang oneself explain

Inner child can be wild

Higher self-blown up elf

Bearing gift above the rift

Energy held dark expelled

Testimony not a phony

To afraid to speak fear of some judge
Judge your own self and what you love

Could be a cat maybe a dog
Doesn't really matter as long as there's love

The heart's desire the return
What's put out not the burn

Categorically speaking it is good
Unconditionally if understand

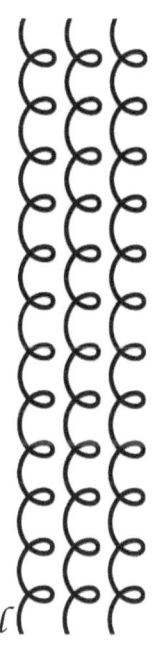

But when bonded to beliefs not of source
The path is changed and goes of course

Cowards rely on complacency
Conformity so we never are free

When we love our own heart we love our soul
Its time to start learning and feel the glow

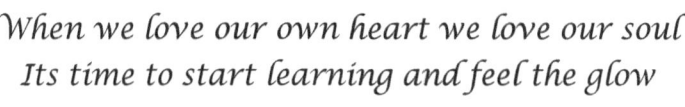

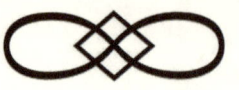 

Loyalty leaving lasting print
Negative energy is from where to sprint

Casting confusion angry plan
Fueling the fire with a fan

Bent on revenge hate inside
Dead on arrival dead inside

Cutters in one hand loyalty other
It's your choice me or mother

Narcissist or honor truth or lies
You're to choose alone despise

What's in heart or what's in mind
Clear in vision or be blind

Your direction belongs to you
Our love can't die because it's true

Another heart break another past
Wasn't meant to ever last

No regrets tried my best
No lost sleep while I rest

Intense emotions turn to calm
Relieved to know I'm moving on

Still have self and my trust
Just another step to polish rust

See the sunshine moving near
As this love I had must disappear

Without anguish without shame
Without worry without blame

What comes next some surprise
Another angle with sparkling eyes

Time invested for a cause
Outside society and its dumb laws

Compass guided moral code
Never alone out on the road

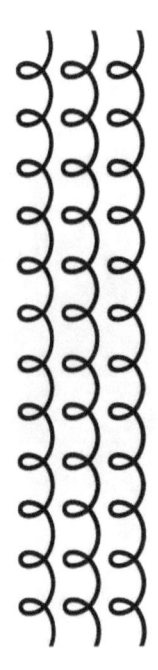

Destination inner peace
Sword in hand to slay any beast

Always willing and aware
Wind be blowing through my hair

Honest angel no matter the pain
Discernment gleaming from every vein

One more gift to enjoy the show
another lesson embrace the glow

Miracle madness everyday
On this path I shall stay

Unconditional or conditional which you pick
One to uplift or keep you sick

Unconditional bond through the heart
Not dependent on any other part

A sacred space within the soul
Allowing love to be in flow

Shared experience an honored way
Through the pain is how we pay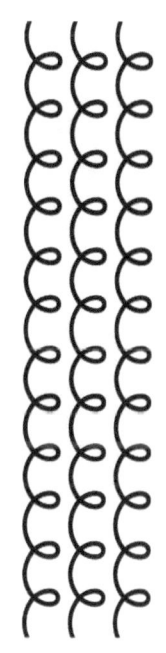

Life's big lessons and the small
A chance to rise up before the fall

Gratitude and grace responsible
For own acts respectable

Taught and learned not from a book
But from the heart that was almost took

Admiration strength within
Rise above a life called sin

Stop sweety look around
See in life what can be found

Be present every moment
Wheel of life is truly woven

Stay open to some change
Let your heart out weigh your brains

Love life all you can
Don't let control destroy your plan

Authority figures come and go
They will try and steal the show

Work hard don't give up
Use your gift fill your own cup

Ride ambition sail through
Hold your head up avoid the blues

Fight your own battles leave there's to them
You're a warrior grow your own stem

More to men than meets the eyes
When we see through all those lies

Endangered list man and more
On false narratives that rot the core

Precisely aimed indigent shrines
Drunk on power and cheap wines

Holy rollers proclaim what's right
White skin demons of the night

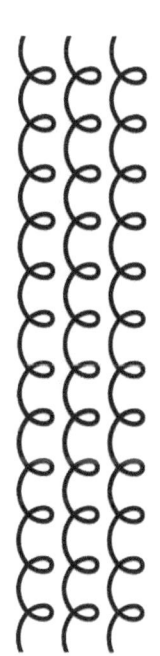

Satanic slaughter spreading fear
Natives starving without dear

Answers coming responsible
Fractured learning of the soul

Truth will ride in honors rain
Someday soon without pain

Laughing through the pain graphic in detail
Off the drugs provided by the whale

Prescription paradise fairy land for sure
Synthetic symbiosis never was a cure

Best face forward shoes are tied
What was the purpose of he who lied

Money backing principals leveraged on our backs
Virtues of the greedy sharpening that ax

Alleged diagnosis accepted way
Dumbing us down numb everyday

Here i stand strong and proud
Wind through my hair on my own cloud

Conformity tried but has failed
That life for me has long since sailed

Frightening and traumatic despite the cause
Religion violates the universe's laws

Spoon feeding fear formula
Brainwashed parents bla bla bla

Characteristics of a cult
Hope your seated for this jolt

Primal emotions left unchecked
Obligation what the heck

Controlled conditioning worships way
Draining us of a joy ass day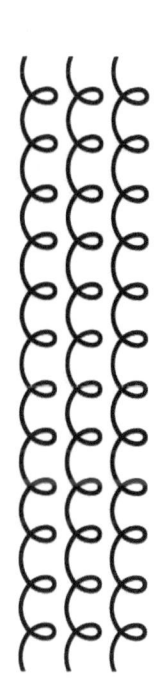

Too afraid to stand out
And seek our truth without doubt

Isn't that what they claim
Power wants us to live in pain

Casteration genocide
Follow the money and you decide

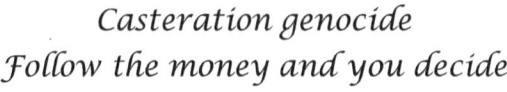

Killing fields left for dead
Back this time for my bread

Retribution has had its price
This time free damn how nice

Intelligent intellect from the street
Raised to rise and defeat

Built and prepped fortified
Here to shock and realize

Hocking loogies to clear my throat
Putting a noose on the goat

Escaped the victim mentality
To find a new reality

It's my turn honored to serve
Smelling the win humanity deserves

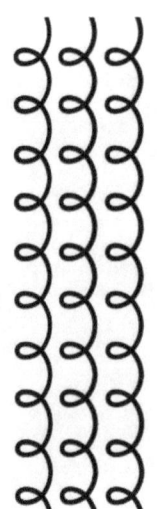

Brainwashed bigots cult mainframe
Eager to point and lay blame

My last feeling ouch that hurt
Rest in peace in the dirt

How 'bout peace in the now
What's that mean and the how

Change the now create a future
One without a doctor's suture

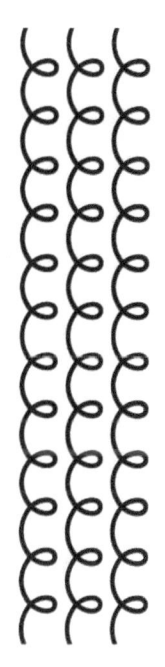

Tourniquet off scar exposed
Slave plantation of the those

Master plan of dastardly deeds
Poisoned are its many seeds

Here's my ass pucker up
Don't need black magic to fill this cup

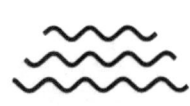

Weak and wounded attracting same
Masters ruling in this plain

Who's fault any how look in the mirror
Until you understand things are clear

Only your truth can set you free
So look inside to become and be

Get out of your way slide into change
Or stay stuck in conformity chains

Slave ships of the financers
Cozy relations for all these years

Dedicated to bleed us dry
Here I spit in your eye

Welcome sign not out front
Your buried burdons have bared the brunt

Held by conditions of others intent
Negative energy heart space been rent

Bewilderment lost looking for love
Praying to angels from heaven above

Crux of the problem religious constraint
Peer shaming fools joyous it ain't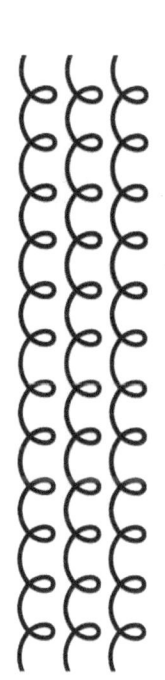

Keep your life not theirs you see
Detach from its grip and exist in the free

Don't let another moment pass you by
Own your own love and feel its high

Love is our purpose love is our bread
Extinguish the lies that live in your head

I'll keep you from falling flat on your face
I'll bring love to your gift you set the pace

No limitations only growth
This I pledge my own oath

Contract in love surrounded by light
Only one tool to win any flight

Preventing poison from my space
Purging tradition dogma displace

Wrestling and restless know my own change
Witnessed the lies that lived in my brains

Seen through the matrix know how it works
Set up and designed by a branch of jerks

What can I say the jerk will soon lose
All things of dark will be singing the blues

Determined already of course not my plan
Just doing my part I do what I can

What doesn't serve the greater good
Are the energies from beneath the dark hood

Casting guilt shame and fear
Are the signal let's be clear

Only dark would emphasize
Negative energies and its lies

False in ego declaring commands
Stripping free will from our hands

Soul of hostage persecute
Never loving not so cute

It's your power take it back
Stand up strong expose the wack

Lean on my love to heal your pain
Find your path learn to explain

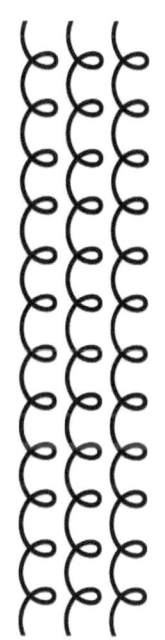

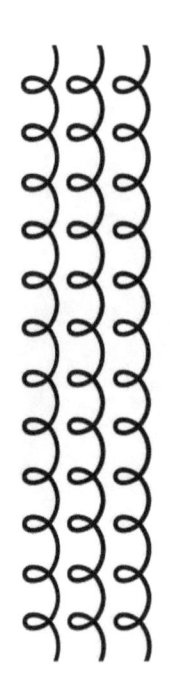

Lofty ambitious false ego fails
Contraband counterfeit lies entails

Men of the power man of the light
Two different meanings much different fight

Portrait of war portrait of love
Choice has a meaning inside and above

Parasites poison love warms the soul
Why has this happened I'll never know

Transcending through space time is not real
Or is the fear the fear you might feel

Pinnacle of life truest in form
The eternal fire that will keep you warm

Or stay trapped in the vomit of pain
It's a choice don't be lame

Master plantation harvesting souls
Locked by contract obligations tolls

Out to lunch dimmer on low
Stagnant passion out of flow

Dangled dollars dreams aside
In the fear as we hide

I got yours if you got mine
Let's break the seal of this new wine

Wishful thinking won't get it done
It's our right to live in fun

Articulate love in how it was meant
Not like the past and how it's been bent

My heart is yours here I stand
Stoke this fire with you fan

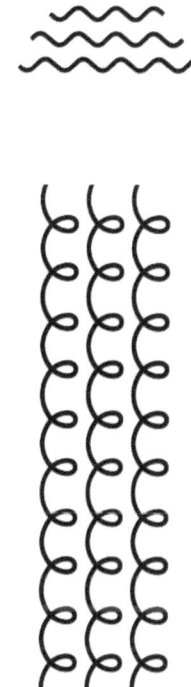

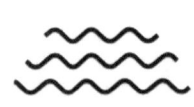

Energy rising to fill in the blank
Washing away what was so dank

Wheels keep turning alluring mind
Defining the reason finding a shine

Content for the moment hostilities clear
Making a plan to get out of here

Back to my people and its warm embrace
Sharing new wisdom all over the place

Open and honest love shining through
Exposed to the light and darkness too

Able to laugh tears from this joy
Birthing a method like a new toy

Eons of capture melting away
Must be my turn to learn, laugh and play

Transformation wow what a change
Lifted to freedom out of the chains

Tell me what happened please share with me
What is it like to be happy and free

Who took the lead what be the source
What kind of teacher teaches this course

Outstanding resemblance of beauty and grace
Obvious from the look of that face

Nice to see you where have you been
Shy in her essence with a cute grin

Heart magic showing eyes a glow
Prepared for the upcoming show

Soul connection to inner sense
High in vibrations so intense

Congratulation welcome to now
Live in the moment share the true how

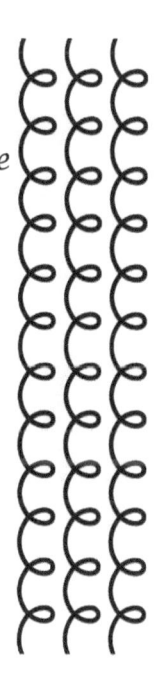

A kind of kindness that has no cost
To ease the suffering of the lost

Heart space magic eternal spark
That lights the way in the dark

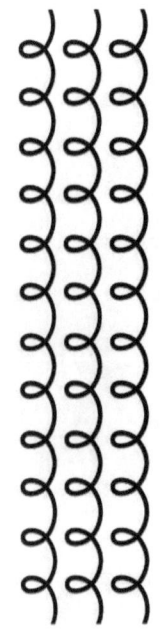

Instilled inspired nurturing
A key that welcomes everything

The start and stop of each day
Free to all there is no pay

A lesson worthy to embrace
Feeling light in this quickened pace

Magnetic examples of what means love
Are our treasures from above

Kind and loving our only hope
Hold on tight to this strong rope

Straining out what doesn't fit
Foible alignment inherited it

Not an excuse accepted no more
The scratching and clawing behind the closed door

An inner world so immense
Here among the lame and dense

Suicidal soldiers destructive drones
Soulless characters of flesh and bones

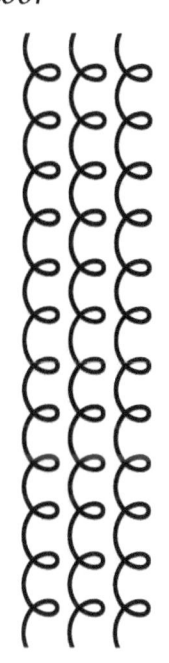

Splintered and fractured no longer real
Toxic intentions you know the deal

Powers plan divide and conquer
Control the narrative quite the wonker

Well just an opinion articulate
Be glad when one moment turns to fate

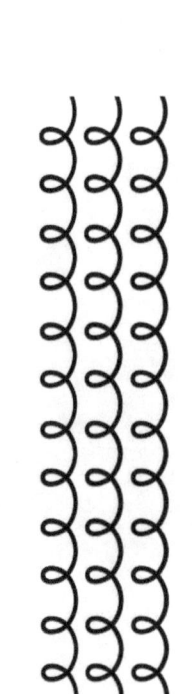

One more question to he who was
Are you proud of what your memory does

Confetti party ticker tape
Legacy of death and rape

Sorry bro but not my fault
Hath what with a grain of salt

Secular symptoms disregard
Destroyed by fear and the tempral tard

Instincts bent dark and cold
A holly whistle that cannot hold

Low vibration separate
Intuition to reveal fate

Sashay left sashay right
Candle burning through the night

Upon each rising new energy flows
Through my being to my toes

Another chance to get this right
To stand in love and avoid the fight

Colorful content spilling out
Filled with wisdom have no doubt

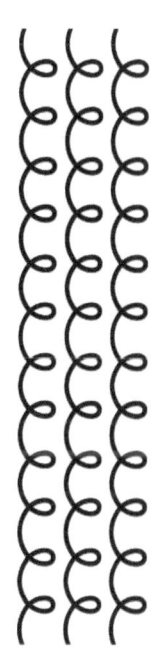

Cocoon to butter beauty in flight
Phosphorus glowing on beaches at night

Partaking in mysteries open receive
Breaking the glass ceiling of the thieves

Pushing forward keeping to self
Being my own man not someone elf

Perilous sometimes positive most
One big thanks to the host

Let us save you from the fear we gave you

Throw yourself in your firey lake
Laugh out loud give me a break

Hostile intentions narrative squed
For the purpose to control me and you

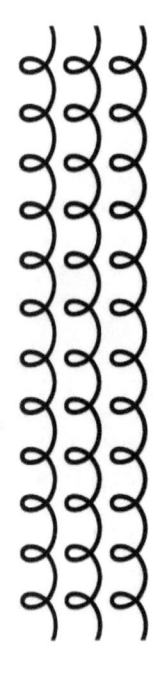

Got it wrong puddin proof
But I do believe in the poof

Alleviate set us free
From a life of conformity

Activate that DNA
The kind who he had in the hay

Leave the week free the meek
Show the passion that we seek

Carry our hearts in one hand
Sound the trumpets of your band

Reversing powers authoritative grip
Greedy scumbags and their trip

Clouding reality configured fires
Meeting shadows untold desires

Strangled hold speaking down
Education of each clown

Impersonation seducing souls
What it robs and untold tolls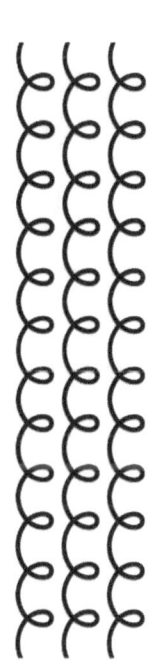

Broken mirror without shine
Ignorance staying drunk on wine

Silly salvation seekers set aside
What you look for is inside

Concocted poison conformity
On your book is where I pee

Dualism case and point
To what the church does annoint

Lost is the sense we've given up
What was meant to fill each cup

Clouded ambitions gone amuck
As the weak and weary pay another buck

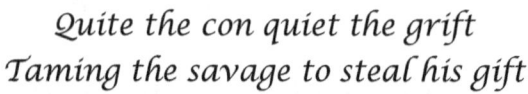

Quite the con quiet the grift
Taming the savage to steal his gift

Banana eating monkeys place in the troop
High on each other buried in poop

Intimidation blackmail strong arm clones
Empty inside except for weak bones

Upright image slithering along
Surrounded now by evolutions song

Tool chest empty war room cleared
Do not accept what fear mongers have feared

Soft sweet whispers in my ear
I hear you calling me home my dear

As I stand here at the edge
This heart of mine I do pledge

To the obese of eternal love
Wings spread wide from above

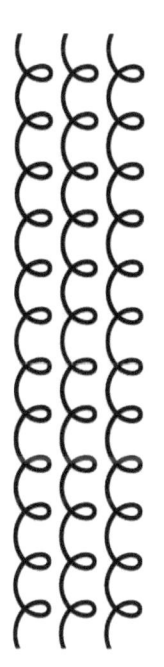

I give to you all I am
In return I'll be your man

Not afraid to see us through
Nothing matters but me and you

Echoed in past lives reminding me
Of this love that's meant to be

No more tears of the pain
Take my hand let love sustain

I see us hugging in my dreams
Our warm embrace lights up scenes

A watchful eye to our fate
All's we need is just one date

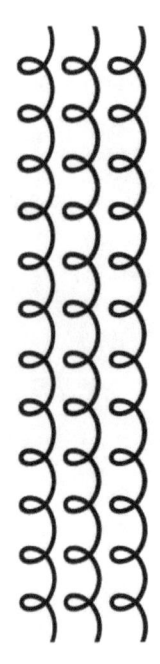

This nurtured union built on love
The heavens gleaming from above

Tested ever time it seems
To find true love and create new dreams

Ever weary from this path
But strong enough for one last gasp

Contact courage explore this realm
It was for you I plant this elm

Sturdy strong deep in root
In you love has what's been put

Immursive expense ready to dance

Recess all day always at play

Seriously detached forcefully hatched

Wisely led back door shed

In plane sight got it right

Powering through societal poo

Shifting gears ringing ears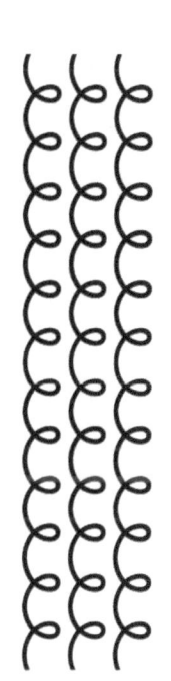

Broken mold so I'm told

Missing link on the brink

Change is near have no fear

Imagination breathes creation

Mystic mind for the grind

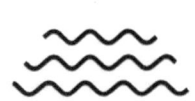

Wealth in love it's our right
Free to find our inner light

Honest intent out of denial
Turning a frown into a smile

Have what we need prepared before birth
To find contentment here on this earth

Satisfaction of a job well done
Under the moon under the sun

Each our own star created to shine
Open your curtain stop being blind

Open to love open to change
At first it might feel real strange

Keep pushing through your gift awaits
Don't be discouraged it's great to feel great

Another day over given what I got
Changing a narrative to what it's not

Light hearted mostly sometimes firm
All of seed needs it's sperm

Proper soil love and water
Destination on the plotter

Soldiering freedom and free will
Without the blinders of evil and kill

What wake up see for yourself
Or stay ignorant elf on a shelf

Conveniently conformed misguided muse
Abusing it's power confined in old shoes

Weak at it core still holding on
Joyous celebration when you are gone

Intimacy without the act
Hearts in love with a pact

Here for you there for me
Destined to be light and free

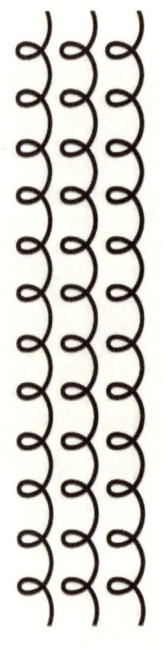

Two four leaf clovers side by side
Sharing the strength they find inside

Virtues morals and respect
With a kiss we call a peck

Love connection unbroken bond
Support coming from beyond

Sing that heart song in my ear
Lift our love above the clear

Sit in silence feel the flow
Light a candle let it glow

Emerald skies glowing bright
Despite inhabitants bread to fight

Your wholesome ego that is warm
That effervescent sense of form

Enveloped essence cradling life
Natures balance through cosmic light

Casim clearing arteries clogged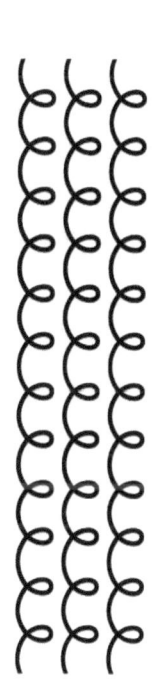
The blind are living it its fog

Paramount pictures Disneyland
Big screen business on demand

Dilutional distractions dead end doom
In our face coming soon

Hidden intentions cover ups
Poking holes in our cups

Energy demons crevasse like traps
Regurgitation of what it craps

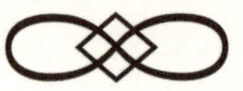 

Boxed in cornered escape route blocked
Head of the rooster gonna get chopped

Wolf crying victims lairiet cut
Noose of nonsense no such luck

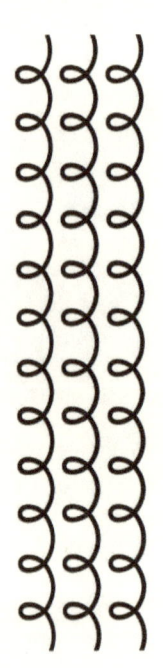

What comes next narratives gone
Doesn't matter I see a new dawn

Oppress a people and find out
What true vengeance is all about

Article of war in the trash
What's that on your face a sickly rash

Harpoons tipped what hate can't take
There is no love of the fake

Open wound here's some salt
Blame yourself it's your own fault

Celebration of expansion
At cost of first nation

Beginning of the end red man's dimise
Not without a fight proud warrior dies

Caticlismic result parasites presue
Rape rob pillage chaos ensue's

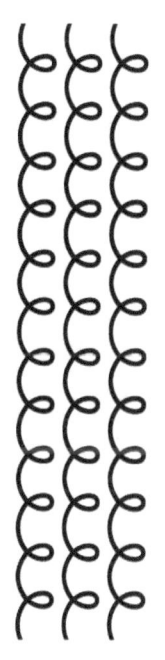

Hide the truth avoid the facts
Disregard he who yields the axe

Gun powder lead alcohol
Small pox blankets relentless brawl

Savagely preserving a way of life
Not able to overcome white men blith

Instinctual liar without trust
Hell bent on murder wealth and lust

Religious right you've been served
What comes next is whats deserved

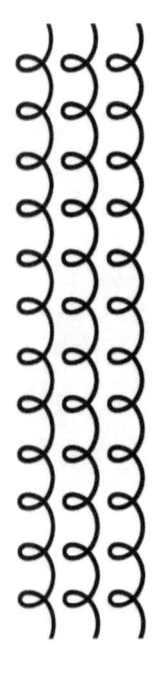

Comemoration of your cult
Nails removed next its bolt

Divided and conquered lusting quest
Unwelcome pessant sick like guest

Arrows piercing through whats said
From your book that's been read

Your way home I'm already here
With my kind whom I love dear

On the winds across the planes
Viral sickness many a strains

Prideless parasite ego false
Without a heartbeat negative pulse

Deficating reflection none
It's your turn to be scared and run

Moving forward in reverse
To clear the six hoax and their curse

Traps lay idle perversely silent
They can't slay this true giant

Eons waiting around the bend
Whatever it takes I won't pretend

From the shadows light shines through
All because of me and you

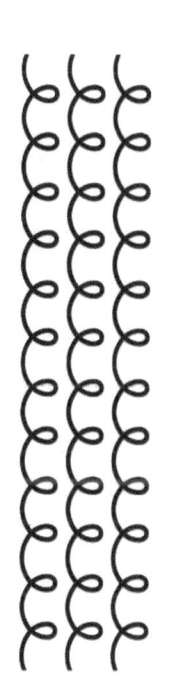

Dirty debris hiding gold
Playing the dice that I hold

One trick pony broken leg
For one's truth one must beg

Torn to shreds ceremoniously
Any thoughts of conformity

My life my soul part the sea
Sit back relax and you shall see

Slipped through some crack or purposely gone
Honesty erased darkening each dawn

Prequisite pictured one sided aloof
Somewhere someone caused a big goof

Wool over eyes wheelchair bound
Hard to believe what can be found

Explanation questions galore
Cracks and crevasses to explore

Fractured framework pissing match
Beneath the surface is where I scratch

Dimensional digging acutely aware
Guided always spiral stair

Circumstantial not so fast
Throttle pegged on the gas

Whimpering whispers won't hold on
Shelter seekers will be gone

Rushing around putting out fires
Created by mersons guns for hire

Strings being pulled shadows do lurk
Uniform needed or going biserk

Showing its hand ignorance prevails
Many have died along its trails

Acclaimed notoriety novality sake
Pitchfork through the chest evils stake

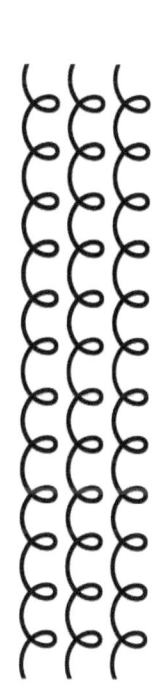

Slander me label me I don't care
With each dish I prepare

Spaghetti and meatballs meatballs alright
High as a J-Bird high as a kite

There's your pedestal here's my axe
Nattered no more like the blacks

Hater do what they are
This message I carry will go far

End of each path where I start
Following only what's in my heart

Stepping with respect always in flow
Existing and learning willing to grow

Never alone never apart
Into the balance like at the start

No rock unturned much more to learn
Why do people think they might burn

Respectably speaking ignorant
Conformity has one intent

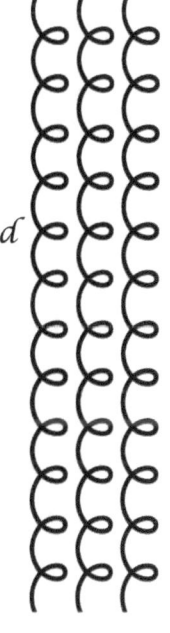

Forging family through good ties
Built on trust not some lies

Birthed through bonding time and again
Karma dies and humanity wins

Influencing each other good or bad
Till someone breaks free then someone is mad

Stay on your path got one of my own
Save your opinion don't call on the phone

I know it hurts it hurts me too
In this moment I still love you

Don't want to lose what's been built
My love for you is full tilt

Time to step back not retreat
Let healing happen from your head to your feet

I've left you full full as I could
Unconditional love as understood

Like a blossoming fruit a fragrant flower
It's your turn to find your true power

Alignment with child and higher self
Control surrendered intuition is wealth

No more plan just to feel love
Free flow within lifted above

I got your back my heart is yours
Here again with many tours

Helping hand with intention
Salvation sickness anil retention

Lied to us for so damn long
Martar model provides the song

Smoke and mirrors don't hold up
To honest truth that fills my cup

Designed to denigrate stifle growth
Obligation to false oath

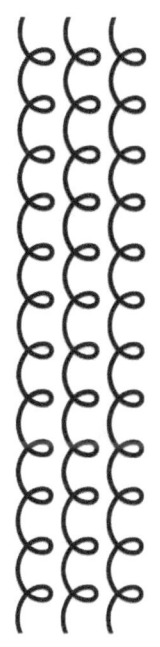

Catering commands not free will
Another poison wrong color pill

Sinful sick lit by fear
What a pain in the rear

Come on people figure it out
I got bombs have no doubt

Projections poison that we ain't good
Evils intention has with stood

Passing on angers hate
Never knowing loves our fate

Adjudication in happiness
Where's the chaos where's the mess

Shady foundations zealous fools
Feed on anger greed and rules

Crooked energy waste of time
Conformity rubbing off your shine

Delirious dilution hurting self
Separation from true wealth

Heart strings tugged once again
Another victim of brainwashed sin

Fleeced of self trapped in lies
Head of falsehoods paralyzed

Harsh projections rally cry
No one's coming it is all a lie

Set in stone THS
Here again for the kiss

Lessons lingered out of touch
This and more there is so much

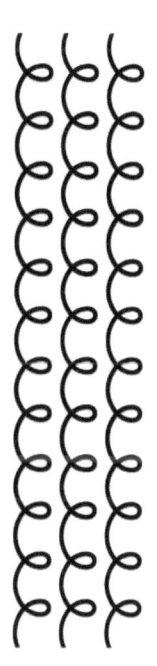

Mirrored image created to shine
Controlling children drunk on wine

Our truest gift forced to conform
Adultism in its highest form

Conditions causing justify
Inside each truth not the lies

Believing in love I stay true
Wanting to experience something new

Under a waterfall breathless shower
In this love is real power

Thoughts of passion set aside
Focus on what lives inside

Visual dreaming not a crime
Not afraid to not be blind

Eyes wide open heart a glow
Love is all I want to know

Wishful thinking don't think so
Through this power I do grow

Living and learning to be free
Without religion and its butchery

Authority figure controlling thought
Leading to sickness maybe a clot

Emotionally deprived separation
Downfall of another nation

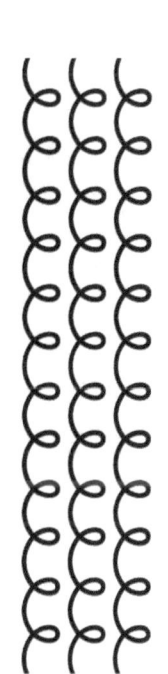

Empires collapsing on themselves
Indignant authority blinding elves

Slavery purpose nothing has changed
Stay in confusion bonded by chains

Scripted and tested narrative non sense
Burden of life in the past tense

Ripened seed of the greed
Tares apart what we really need

Appreciation after respect
Horse before the cart what the heck

Firey friction stories told
To a conscience does it hold

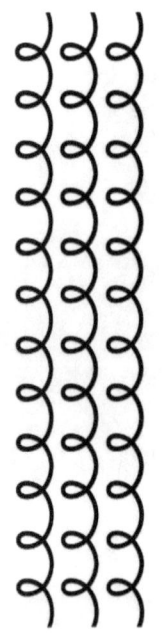

Candle to the light arbitrary
What I find can be scary

Stage is set no trial run
Glad I'm me cuz I have fun

No U-turn light and lite
Negative runs childlike fit

Acting out what it knows
Conformity and all its tolls

Oxie moron widdled down
Propped on lies in every town

Long standing union heaven on earth
From conception of each birth

Not my plan but what I love
Channeling messages that are of

Our growth in wisdom destroyed by fools
Ignorance of the tools

Ancient memories do reside
Given daily do provide

Answers ringing in my ears
All the ones I've know for years

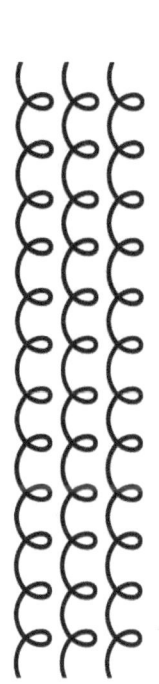

Augmented lies told and re
Burdened pain and misery

Foolish rules supporting lies
Powers purpose conformitys guise

Conform or be cast out what a line
Who's at your table as you dine

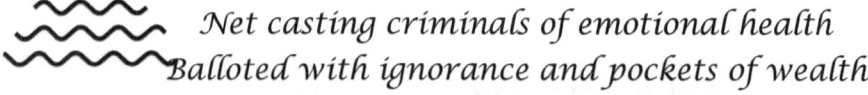

Net casting criminals of emotional health
Balloted with ignorance and pockets of wealth

Material seduction clawing away
Moral erosion power play

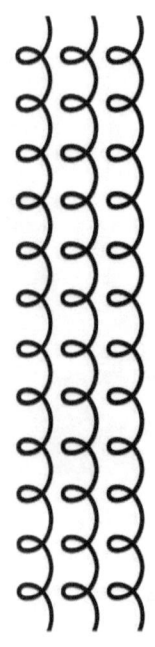

Dignity cloaked intent understood
Should I not or should I should

Peace offering no not a chance
Keep your olives and its broken branch

No longer your narrative out of the way
Wolf crying scapegoat serpents stay

Kill all the children one hath been born
Recorded atrocity just like porn

Sick and sad of the mad
Power collapsing and that's rad

Moral men hold your breath
Hold your possessions close to your chest

Liberation independence crown
Casting shadows upon your frown

Backwards remnants poisoned past
Smoldering embers here's your gas

Murderous felons hitch hiking fools
Days are numbered for these tools

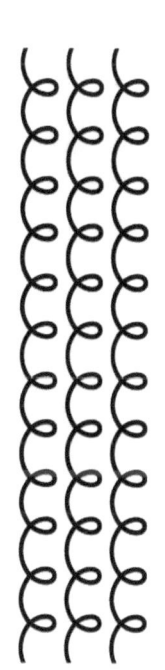

Galaxy giving guidance clear
Green light go love is the river

Dedication ripples grow
Energy building for the big show

Dunce cap on not an excuse
Guilt by association and its abuse

Mocking the parrot repeating lies
Without feathers this bird dies

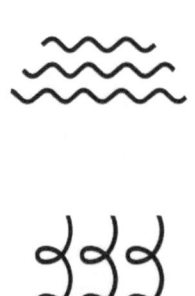

Red and believed history's past
Colorful characters quiet the cast

Rescuers saviors prophetic punch
Leaving its readers out to lunch

Supertrap in the gap
What the huh holly crap

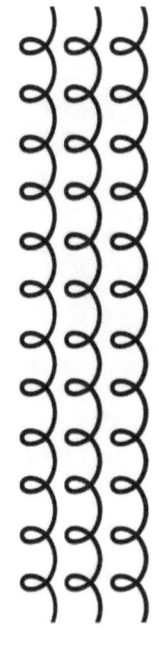

White bread nonsense coexist
Secret names on its list

Frozen fingers steelie hearts
Injecting poison with its darts

Satisfaction with our pain
Obstruction present in your lane

Priest and deacon don't supersede
What we really really need

Wisdoms window in each soul
Tell the church just where to go

*Sparkling heart is what I see
In each moment we are free*

*Confusion cast out projections gone
Others opinions are a yawn*

*Showtime baby cameras roll
No more narcissist no more toll*

*Motion picture of all time
Humoror within every line*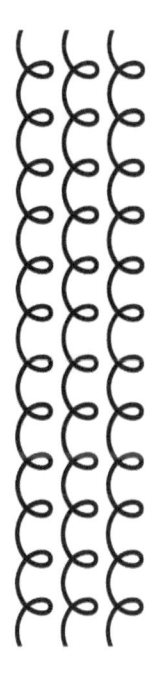

*How the soul was meant to be
On conformity is where we pee*

*Master courage gather strength
Don't get caught up in the ranks*

*It's our turn we are one
Uptight bitch*s aren't no fun*

*Go ahead make my day
Triggering fools is how I play*

Situation salvation give me a break
Ignorance bread forged by the fake

Independence gone co-dependence thrives
Altered vision of the hive

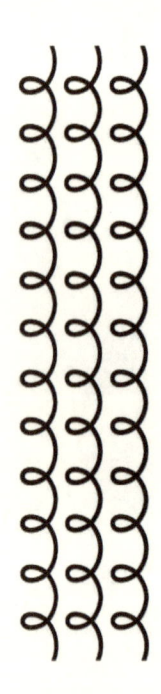

Permitting every pore
Scaring all that I adore

Envy cuz you'll never be free
Jealousy cuz you're not me

Hear this message don't be numb
Against conformity don't succumb

Blasted daily low in vibe
Causing chaos along the ride

Conclusion reaching pain not love
We all the one we all that dove

Rule one out of the way
Not gonna have a negative day

Rule two question why
Is it conformity and part of the lie

Rule three exist and be free

Rule four step through each new door

Rule five burn down the hive

Rule six only love can fix

Rule seven enjoy your own heaven

Rule eight stay focused and straight

Rule nine polish to shine

Rule ten start over gain

The perfect print of passions grace
In each soul of this race

Inner reflection who we are
Time to heal long lasting scar

Each a star prideful and pure
Despide false narrative meant to smeer

Thankful and grateful to have this chance
Prosper in love and feel a new dance

Odds stacked against no longer concerned
Can't give up on what makes me burn

Triggered past lives casting doubt
On what reality is all about

Indoctrination to dark energy cause
Martyrs dying to unjust laws

Lambs blood trinity 70 wives
Rhetoric division senseless lives

Trapped in projection false in path
Apparently victims of God's rath

Not true at all just a hoax
Powers enslavement of us folks

Please hear me out watch power squirm
Back to its hole just like a worm

Power corrupts empires fall
I be laughing having a ball

Can't touch this so don't even try
Liars are criminals no matter the why

To: A Thought Provoking Friend

Do gooder doing for a cause
Saving their ass's off commanded by laws

Wipe your window see through the glair
No one was ever standing there

Redundancy written into each soul
Sick on the poison swallowed it whole

More better hostage took from the wild
Taming the beast making it mild

Suffering savages we are still here
Conformity can't kill us neither can beer

Fight with our wisdom fight with our heart
This is our time to get set apart

Align with our guides presence strong
High in vibration singing our song

Take back our power stand in our truth
Empty the coverns of all stolen loot

www.ingramcontent.com/pod-product-compliance
Lightning Source LLC
LaVergne TN
LVHW041712060526
838201LV00043B/690